REINDEER

written by Emery Bernhard

illustrated by Durga Bernhard

HOLIDAY HOUSE · NEW YORK

For our friends
at the
Woodstock Library

Library of Congress Cataloging-in-Publication Data
Bernhard, Emery.
Reindeer / written by Emery Bernhard ; illustrated by Durga
Bernhard. — 1st ed.
p.   cm.
ISBN 0-8234-1097-8
1. Reindeer—Juvenile literature.   [1. Reindeer.]   I. Bernhard,
Durga, ill.   II. Title.
QL737.U55B52   1994   93-45327   CIP   AC
599.73'57—dc20

Special thanks to Robin Dalton, Curator of Animals,
Queens Wildlife Center, New York State Zoological
Society/The Wildlife Conservation Society, for his
comments on the text and artwork.

Every year at Christmas, people tell the story of the flying reindeer that pull Santa's sleigh through the winter sky. Have you ever wondered about the real reindeer? What do we know about these unique deer of the far north?

MALE REINDEER

Reindeer are found in Scandinavia, Alaska, Canada, Greenland, and the former Soviet Union. In North America, reindeer have been given the name caribou.

FEMALE CARIBOU

Reindeer are constantly on the move, seeking new pastures, fleeing from bad weather, and escaping from enemies. Most other kinds of deer never stray far from the place where they are born.

Like all deer, reindeer have antlers. Antlers are the strong, branching bones that grow out of a deer's skull. Both male and female reindeer have antlers. In other types of deer, only the male grows them.

Antlers have sharp points and can be good weapons for fighting off a wolf, coyote, or another deer. Pregnant females sometimes use their antlers to drive other reindeer away from the food they need to eat.

New antlers begin as soft, swelling knobs that are coated with tender, hairy skin called velvet.

Each year, deer antlers fall off and then grow back again. Male reindeer, called bulls, shed their antlers in November and December, after

When antlers stop growing, the velvet dries up and peels off. A deer polishes its hardened, bony antlers by rubbing them against branches and bushes.

mating season. The female reindeer, called cows, keep their antlers until May or June, shedding them at about the same time they give birth to their calves. Two weeks later, the new antlers start to grow in.

In the spring and fall, reindeer gather in large herds. In the spring, they travel northward to reach their summer feeding grounds. In the fall, they return to the scrubby forests of the south where they again find food and shelter from bitter winter storms.

These seasonal journeys are called migrations. Reindeer migrate up to 1,600 miles each year.

Reindeer gather on the slope of a hill in the far north. Wind roars over the barren winter landscape, sweeping the rocky slope almost free of snow. The reindeer nibble on tough plants, called lichens, that grow in thick tufts along the frozen ground.

Reindeer have broad, flat hooves and dewclaws that come close to the ground. They give sure footing on snow and mud. Reindeer hooves also help reindeer paddle along when they swim.

DEWCLAWS

In the long northern winter, food is scarce. Reindeer who do not find enough to eat will starve. Although they try to graze where plants are exposed, reindeer must be able to reach lichens, mosses, and other plants even when they are buried underneath deep snow. Reindeer use their sharp-edged hooves to scrape away the snow that covers their food.

When snow piles up in deep drifts, reindeer browse on tree twigs, evergreen branches, and the lichen growing on trees. Reindeer have small, weak teeth, and spend much time chewing. Like other deer, they have special stomachs that break down plants that are hard to digest. Reindeer eat about 12 pounds of food per day. They can grow up to 7 feet in length and have an average weight of 350 pounds.

It is May in the Arctic. The sun is strong, and the few remaining snow-drifts are melting. A herd of 4,000 reindeer clatters down a rocky trail toward a wide lake. As the reindeer walk, the bones in their feet make a loud clacking noise. They walk close to each other, grunting and snorting and knocking their antlers together. The reindeer are skinny and their winter coats are shedding. They have been traveling north up to 35 miles a day since the middle of March.

The reindeer are good swimmers. When they reach the far side of the lake, they begin to spread out over the vast treeless plains of the Arctic.

This swampy open land, where the soil beneath is always frozen, is called tundra. The reindeer have arrived at their summer grazing grounds.

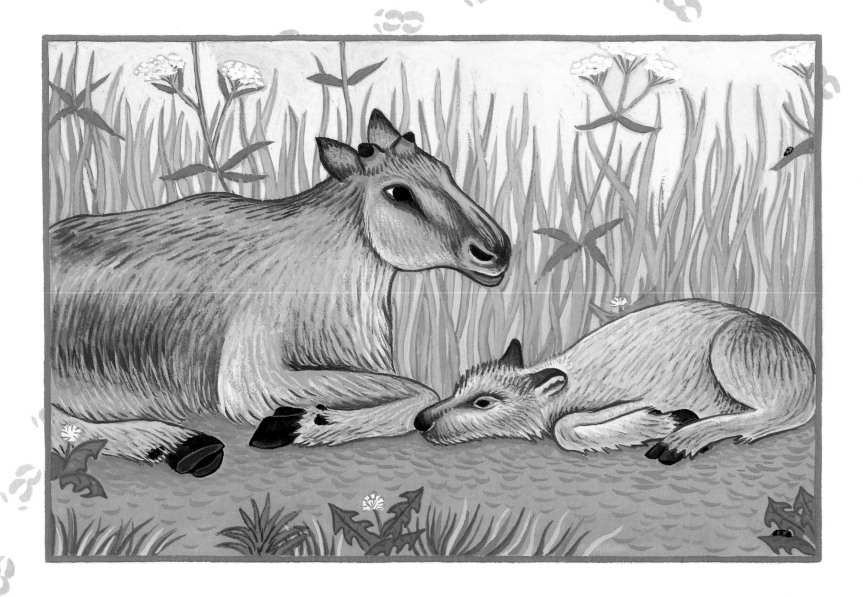

It is time for the calves to be born. Pregnant reindeer cows look around nervously. After giving birth, a new mother lies beside her baby, nudging and licking it. Then she stands and moves a few feet away, urging her newborn to get up. The reindeer calf tries to stand on quivering legs, falls down, and finally wobbles to its feet again. It is 2 feet long and weighs about 13 pounds.

The calf stays close to its mother. For one year, it will follow her wher-ever she roams. Wolves may hunt down any calf that is weak or strays from the protection of the herd.

Reindeer calves nurse often, gaining strength from their mother's rich, nourishing milk. Two days after it is born, a calf can keep up with the adults. After ten days, it weighs about 26 pounds. In two months, calves must be ready to migrate to the herd's winter grounds.

During the short arctic summer, the reindeer rest and feed and gain weight. They eat lichens, mosses, marsh grasses, willow leaves, blueberry bushes, and mushrooms. The reindeer move from place to place in small herds, eating plants in one grazing area before moving on to another.

But warm weather does not mean an easy life on the tundra. Huge swarms of insects bite the reindeer. On windless days, flies, gnats, and mosquitoes are so annoying that the reindeer may panic and try to run away.

With the coming of fall and the first cold nights, the reindeer become restless. Their coats grow long and dense. They begin to drift south.

In November, mating season begins. The male reindeer try to attract and mate with as many female reindeer as they can. The bulls fight any other males who come near. They rush about and bellow and clash their antlers together. This is called rutting.

After the rut, the reindeer again gather in large herds for the southward migration. Winter is coming to the tundra. The pregnant cows will carry their growing calves inside their wombs for eight months, until they return to their summer grazing grounds in June.

Reindeer fur is made of long, hollow hairs that stand out from the skin and cover the short, curly underfur. Because these hairs are filled with air, they keep reindeer warm and help them stay afloat in water.

Reindeer run away from wolves, bears, hunters, and the biting insects of summer, but they do not seem bothered by the cold. Their thick, shaggy fur traps a thick layer of warm air around their bodies. Reindeer fur insulates so well that falling snow doesn't melt on their backs. Even on a frigid day, a galloping reindeer will quickly become overheated and begin panting.

In warm weather, reindeer may climb into the mountains not just to escape from the biting insects of the lowlands, but also to wallow in the cooling snow of the high peaks.

ANTLER
ARROWHEADS

REINDEER
SKIN
TENT

GLOVE
EMBROIDERED
WITH REINDEER
HAIR

REINDEER-HIDE
PARKA

SPOON CARVED
FROM ANTLER

Fifty thousand years ago, reindeer were painted on the walls of sacred caves. For at least that long, humans have hunted reindeer, and not just for their meat.

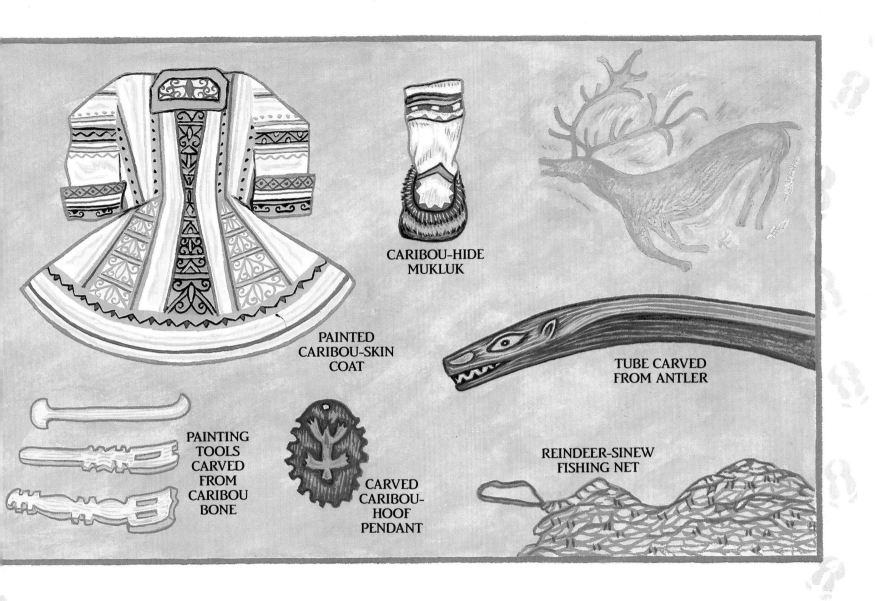

CARIBOU-HIDE
MUKLUK

PAINTED
CARIBOU-SKIN
COAT

TUBE CARVED
FROM ANTLER

PAINTING
TOOLS
CARVED
FROM
CARIBOU
BONE

CARVED
CARIBOU-
HOOF
PENDANT

REINDEER-SINEW
FISHING NET

Reindeer fur has also been used to keep humans warm. Jackets, hoods, leggings, boots, and tents have been made from the hides and skin. Reindeer fat has been burned in lamps at night. The antlers have been used to make needles, knife handles, sled runners, fishhooks, and other tools.

Within the last several thousand years, the people of northern Asia and Europe learned to live on the move, following the reindeer that provided their food, clothing, and shelter. They caught the cows and milked them. They protected their herds from wolves and rounded up reindeer when they ran away. Some reindeer were trained to carry riders and to pull sleighs across the snow. Reindeer can pull 300-pound loads up to 50 miles a day at a speed of about 15 miles per hour.

A few reindeer owners in Scandinavia and the former Soviet Union still follow their herds on their migrations. Others truck herds from pasture to pasture, and ride snowmobiles instead of reindeer sleds.

In modern times, reindeer have faced increased hunting and the loss of their wide open ranges as dams, highways, and oil pipelines have been built. Where there were once as many as 10 million reindeer in the northlands, there are now fewer than 500,000.

REINDEER-HIDE
DRUM AND
DRUMSTICK

Long ago, tribal peoples of the north believed that both humans and animals had magical powers, and they told tales of people flying off to other worlds on sleighs drawn by reindeer. Did the idea for Santa's nighttime journey come from these ancient stories? No one knows. We do know that the gentle reindeer is popular with children around the world.

Although reindeer have a place in petting zoos and cattle corrals and Christmas stories, their real home is in the wild.

Glossary

antlers: the strong branching bones that grow out of a deer's skull.

bulls: male adult reindeer.

calves: young immature reindeer.

caribou (KAR-i-boo): North American reindeer.

cows: female adult reindeer.

dewclaw: a small toe on the reindeer's leg that comes low to the ground in walking and helps keep the animal from sinking in mud and snow.

insulate (IN-su-layt): to cover or protect with something that prevents the loss of heat.

lichen (LIE-ken): tough, dry-looking plants that grow in thick tufts on solid surfaces like rocks, trees, and frozen ground.

migration (mi-GRAY-shun): the seasonal movement from one place to another for feeding or mating.

mukluk (MUK-luk): a boot made out of reindeer skin or sealskin and worn by the Inuit.

parka (PAR-ka): a hooded jacket made from caribou fur and worn by the Inuit.

rut: the time each year, usually in the fall, when male deer compete with each other to mate with female deer.

sinew (SIN-yoo): the strong white strands of flesh that connect muscles to bones in animals, and that can be dried and used as cord, thread, fishing line, bowstrings, and many other things.

tundra (TUN-dra): vast, level, treeless plains of the Arctic where the soil underneath is always frozen.